DOGS

MAKE US HUMAN

To the dogs in my life, who taught me the meaning of love.

—Jeffrey Moussaieff Masson

For Delilah, Murdo, Petra, Vinnie, River, Ruby, and Malti.

—Art Wolfe

DOGS MAKE

US HUMAN

A GLOBAL FAMILY ALBUM

JEFFREY MOUSSAIEFF MASSON AND ART WOLFE

BLOOMSBURY

NEW YORK · BERLIN · LONDON · SYDNEY

Published by Bloomsbury USA, New York

All papers used by Bloomsbury USA are natural, recyclable products made from wood grown in well-managed forests. The manufacturing processes
conform to the environmental regulations of the country of origin.

LIBRARY OF CONGRESS CATALOGING-IN-PUBLICATION DATA HAS BEEN APPLIED FOR.
ISBN: 978-1-60819-565-7

First U.S. edition 2011

1 3 5 7 9 10 8 6 4 2

Designed by Lauren Jantz

CONTENTS

INTRODUCTION
by Jeffrey Moussaieff Masson

The great revelation of Art Wolfe's spectacular photos in this book is that the love of dogs is not limited to the Western world. Dogs are to be found everywhere, from Manhattan to Mongolia. There is not a single landmass that does not contain dogs, and dogs living, for the most part, with people. Our relationship with dogs is the single most important symbiotic relationship between humans and another species on the planet, the most delightful, and in many ways still the most mysterious. We can never expect to understand it completely, but we are certainly getting closer each day.

The special bond we share is one that seems to confer, to borrow a phrase from evolutionary biology, survival benefits on both species. Humans, as endless studies remind us, live longer and healthier lives in the company of dogs. Patients in a hospice, a cancer unit, or a burn center all do better when dogs come to visit. As a former Freudian psychoanalyst, I have always claimed that just about any dog would make a better therapist than just about any human. You hope your therapist is not too interested in your status, your color, your money, your social

USA. Yellowstone National Park, Wyoming. *(left)* Coyote *(Canis latrans)*.

Chile. Torres del Paine National Park. Argentine gray fox (*Pseudalopex griseus*) nursing kits.

class, but you can be absolutely certain that your dog is not. The biases, prejudices, and presuppositions of humans are foreign to dogs. They love us just as we are. They adore us, in fact. They crave our presence.

Dogs make us fully human. They awaken us to many of the qualities we find in them that we wish to have in ourselves. We wish to be loyal and forgiving and loving. We wish to be focused on important things like family, enjoying time in the wild, walking in the woods, being with friends, lying about indolently in the sunshine. We would like to believe we could make friends with anyone if we try hard enough, to believe that we neither have nor need to have enemies at all in the world. Dogs by and large cannot pass another dog on the street without indicating the interest that we might feel were we alone on earth—and suddenly discovered there was one

other human present. Dogs seem to feel this intense interest *all* the time. Their sniffing is the equivalent of our taking the time to stop and gossip, something we only do when we know the person. But dogs "know" all other dogs, as it were, simply by virtue of belonging to the same species. When my dog is in the car, sitting in the front seat looking out the window, and he suddenly sees another dog on the street or in a car, he is frantic to let me know, "Look, look, there is another dog there! Another dog! Wow! Please stop so that I can introduce myself."

Dogs have a gene that has a human counterpart that can only be found in children with Williams syndrome, in whom the gene causes exceptional gregariousness. Strange coincidence, is it not? These children—small, gentle, elflike in appearance—are remarkably sociable. They chat and make friends and show no aggressive tendencies. So is it possible that dogs simply have a gene for liking to be around others and us? (I mean this metaphorically of course.) And that missing that gene, we find ourselves attracted to it in dogs? Because otherwise it is hard to explain why humans, so different from one another from culture to culture around the globe, are equally attracted to dogs. There is no other animal who has this universal effect.

The question of how long dogs and humans have been together and how this special relationship began has been a subject of fascination and study. Robert Wayne, a researcher in Evolutionary Biology from the University of California at Los Angeles, believes that long before we knew dogs, while we were still hunters and gatherers, wolves began to follow small bands of humans. Why? Well, we dog lovers would say they were already attracted to us as a species. But most scientists would agree with Wayne that the wolves were originally scavengers. They followed humans to feed on the prey we wounded but could not kill, or to feed on the carcasses we left behind. Of course, a case could easily be made the other way around: that we were the scavengers, feeding off the more successful hunters' prowess.

Recently there has been a fundamental rethinking of human origins. In the 1960s, "man the hunter" had been the leading hypothesis of how we spent our early time on earth, but this theory has become scientifically threadbare. There are few, if any, researchers who believe it any longer. Instead, scientists are looking much harder at the origins of cooperation— not only between the sexes, but between the species of humans and dogs as well. At first this was thought of as a simple recognition that wolves and humans hunted together. And it is true that dogs enjoy hunting with humans, that is, those dogs who like to hunt, and those humans who feel the same way. The coordinated actions are easy for dogs to understand, perhaps because wolves are already a species that hunts cooperatively. The symbiosis goes even deeper than just hunting, though. Dogs not only helped us find food, they also helped us guard the children and play with them. They alerted us to the arrival of enemies. They even behaved like canine soldiers if the need to fight ever arose. In other words, they more or less "identified" with humans as part of their pack, becoming so essential to early human society that the two species came to reflect each other's qualities. Dogs were us.

In Wayne's scenario, at some stage a group of wolves, perhaps smaller and less fearful than most, developed a dependency on human groups. They were no longer independent hunters, but instead were becoming part of a human band. What would we have gotten in return? Well, according to just about all scholars, we would have a warning system against other predators, or even a means of scaring off other wolves. Wolves are territorial, and if a human band were in their home territory, the wolves would have wanted to see it defended. This period of being protected by wolves could have gone on for several thousand years. However, once settled communities started to appear in the Middle East around fifteen thousand years ago, humans began to intervene in the breeding patterns of their "camp followers," turning them into the first proto-dogs. Humans preferred the

3

Peru. Tambopata-Candamo Reserve. Short-eared dog (*Atelocynus microtis*).

smaller sized ones—and selected for this trait, as it would signal less aggressive intent and be easier to manage in an animal not quite yet a "pet."

Wayne says, "I think a long history such as that would explain how a large carnivore, which can eat you, eventually became stably incorporated in human society." While I agree with his theory, I think it leaves out a far more fundamental event: the psychological incorporation of the dog into the human psyche. *That* is the enduring mystery that this book seeks to plumb, in part by simply calling attention to it in these remarkable photographs. And what is most astonishing about these photos is that aside from our attire—and the dogs'—in some of them, they could have been taken *at any point in the last fifteen thousand years!*

This occurs to me when I lovingly gaze upon my ninety-pound yellow lab, Benjy, as he yawns lazily, displaying to me the mouth of an apex predator—huge teeth that could easily destroy a human in a flash. If dogs saw humans as prey, we would stand no chance against a large one, at least without weapons. But in fact Benjy would no more think of eating me than I would think of eating him. I can allow toddlers to put their hands into his large mouth and not even give a thought to any danger. How strange, when you think about it, that we have created an animal who is so close to us that we trust him or her as much as we trust any other member of our own species. It works both ways too. I am happy to allow Benjy to lie down next to a newborn, and I know that no harm will come to her. (Although many mothers might hesitate, I know.) It is also true that almost any dog who gives birth to puppies in our home happily allows us to touch them and kiss them and make a fuss over them. In fact, she seems to positively revel in our attention. What other animal trusts us sufficiently to want us to be around her young?

Whether the time line is forty thousand years as some investigators believe, or fifteen thousand years, which seems to be emerging as the consensus figure, we have been associated with canines far longer than with any other animal. Also, with the exception of the cat, canines are the only animals we associate with who we have not directly exploited. What I mean is that in the case of dogs we "use" talents and skills they already possess, and the dogs enjoy engaging in them. This is very different from the way we exploit other animals, say the animals who live on farms and are there not because we admire them or want to associate with them as companions, but because we humans want something from them that they would rather not give: their flesh, their fur, their milk, their eggs, their young.

On the other hand, we encouraged dogs to become part of our lives because we like being around them. And they too like being around us. I find it hard to believe that we forced this on dogs. We merely noted a strange propensity on their part to tolerate us early on. And that tolerance turned quickly into affection—and love. That has not changed in fifteen thousand years either.

There are hunter/gatherer societies today in which dogs live with humans and have no other function than to give pleasure. The San tribe from Namibia (famous from the well-intentioned but misleading film *The Gods Must Be Crazy*) certainly hunts with dogs, but that is only for a short part of the day. Most of the time they just hang out with their dogs, which is perhaps why the anthropologist Marshall Sahlins claimed that theirs is a "Zen economy." That is to say their affluence consists of the treasure of their various easygoing relationships, foremost among them the one they have with their dogs. The dogs have no duties. And yet they are not just tolerated; they are celebrated. They don't "belong" to anyone, because hunter-gatherers, like early humans before agriculture, do not have a sense of ownership. They are an intimate part of the life of the band. The dogs are free to go and come, but there is no place they would rather be than with the humans. When the tribe decides to move on, the dogs go as well. There is no question of leaving them behind. (Would you leave one of the children behind?) There is a story of a band where one of the dogs was badly crippled, and could not keep up with the group. He was placed in a sling and carried by different members of the group as they walked to their new home.

The pictures in this book show us something that we already know, but can never contemplate enough: Dogs go with us wherever we go. We have no other relationship with any other animal—even cats—that remotely resembles that between humans and dogs. I live with cats, and adore them, but it is in the very nature of a cat to refuse to relinquish entirely its independence. You can only get so close to a cat before the cat will revert to some extent back to its natural state, which is that of a solitary animal who does not need others in order to exist happily. It is hard to deny the essential difference between dogs and cats in their relations to us: Dogs are completely ours; cats remain true to themselves alone.

Unlike just about any other relationship like this, dogs *want* to be part of the human family. Freud wondered in vain what women really want. But it is easy to answer what dogs really want: They want to live with us and be with us on a constant basis. They cannot get enough of us. Hanging out with humans is the very essence of being a dog. Deprived of a human, a dog looks lonely, bereft, and incomplete. They long for our presence as much as dog lovers long for theirs. Most people who have loved a dog want never to live without one. It becomes a part of one's identity: Jeff and his dogs. Surely this is why among the earliest burial sites we find dogs buried with their human friends.

How does one account for such a strange symbiotic relationship, one that is unquestionably unique in nature? It is not that we *need* dogs, or that dogs *need* humans. Both species do fine on their own. But dogs enhance humans, as much as humans enhance dogs. We enrich their lives just as they enrich ours. It is perhaps the only example in all of nature of pure mutualism. Each party benefits. It is the opposite of what one finds with parasites. But putting it like this by no means conveys the depth or complexity of this symbiosis. For that, we need to think about the feelings involved. It is very hard to explain this to people who have never lived with a dog. They just don't get it. For them, the relationship between humans and dogs remains on a cognitive level; it is a matter of what we *think* about dogs, not what we *feel* about dogs or an individual dog. They are rightly puzzled, because it is impossible to describe the relationship unless there is direct experience; it is like trying to explain the color blue to somebody born blind. But that has not stopped people from trying to fathom the dog/human bond, and this may be because it tells us something essential about our own nature.

There are people who claim that dogs have allowed us to become who we are as a species. How can that be? I think the mystery is clarified when we recognize how deep the human desire is for reaching across the species barrier. We imagine being visited by space aliens, and how that would change our entire perspective of life on earth. But aliens are with us every day: They sleep in our beds. They walk with us. They lick our faces and the faces of our children every morning when we wake up. An alien loves us. And we love that alien in return. Because dogs satisfy our deep desire to be in the presence of another species, to look into the eyes of another species and see mirrored the same affection we feel.

How can we explain the deep bond between dogs and humans—two species that are not even in the same family? We are similarly fascinated with our fellow primates, chimpanzees. But we have never domesticated them and cannot live with them for very long without suffering an act of aggression. One distinction is that humans and canines, but not humans and chimps, have a similar familial setting: Pups are very important to wolf society, and all members of the pack help in caring for them, whether it be babysitting or finding food or simply playing with them. Just as with us, both males and females share the burden and the joy of raising the pups. Male chimps, on the other hand, are far less interactive with their young than the females. Another and far more important reason for our bond with dogs is that they make it clear that they adore us. Chimps certainly do not. Not even wolves do—at least as a species—and this is precisely what we have gained by having domesticated the wolf into the dog. A tame wolf can be a good friend, but he will always remain an unreliable friend. He is still wild, and can at any moment turn against you, his friend, for reasons you may never understand. This will not happen with your dog. Dogs have come from wolves, to be sure, but they are no longer wolves; and people who wish to keep wolves as if they were dogs are in for trouble. People who adopt wolves do so only when the wolves are either born in captivity or have been captured. I know of no instance in which an adult wild wolf has sought out the company of a human for the sheer friendship value in it. I recently saw for the third time the remarkable film by Werner Herzog about Timothy Treadwell, the man who befriended grizzly bears in Alaska, or thought he did, until one of them killed both him and his girlfriend. He was not entirely deluded; nobody has ever lived longer in the presence

of these magnificent creatures than Timothy Treadwell. But while he said over and over in the film how much he loved the bears, it was clear that not one of the bears returned this love. They tolerated him, which in itself is a miracle. He lived without injury every summer for sixteen years in the presence of these large and dangerous animals. But what I found most fascinating in the movie was something that Treadwell seems not to have appreciated for its full value. As far as I know it is the first time we see a spontaneous friendship develop between a human and a completely wild animal: A fox takes a liking to Treadwell, and begins to follow him around. Soon you see in the film that they are spending long languid afternoons

Canada. Gray wolves (*Canis lupus*).

together, and Treadwell is able to stroke the fox, which enjoys the petting exactly as would a dog. Eventually she brings her kits over to meet him as well. But, alas, Treadwell did not put his energy into understanding and enjoying his unique relationship with this totally wild animal. In fact, as far as I am aware, no other canid—that is, member of the dog family—has ever sought out the company of a human in this way, except perhaps the original domesticated wolves.

Dogs want to be with us; they want to share as much of our lives as we allow them to. Eating next to us, sleeping beside us, going on excursions with us—there is hardly an activity that dogs are excluded from. Everywhere in the world, we want to be around them as much as they want to be around us.

What is the psychological explanation for this? Is it because dogs remind us that we too are just one more animal species on the planet, and living with them keeps us humble? Or do they satisfy some urgent need for what E. O. Wilson and others have called "biophilia," the need to stay connected with the natural world that surrounds us? This appears to be especially important for children who spontaneously form intense, deep bonds with their pets, and in particular with the dog in the family. I have seen it in my two sons, now age fourteen and nine: A larger, stronger being wants to be your best friend! Take away a child's puppy, and you have dealt that child a blow from which she may never recover.

The depth of affection dogs have for us never fails to startle, on a daily basis. "How come this being loves me so much more than he loves him-self?" That, surely, is at the very heart of the mystery of dogs. We hope that reading this book and looking at Art Wolfe's breathtaking images of humans and dogs living together will help to clarify and celebrate this enchanting mystery.

I believe that the single most endearing trait of dogs is that they do not make the kinds of us/them distinctions that humans routinely engage in. Not for dogs: Where are you from? What language do you speak? What color are you? Ethnicity? Religion? Class? None of these arbitrary distinctions we humans routinely make matters in the least. For dogs, each dog is merely a dog—or rather essentially a dog—and for that very reason *infinitely* interesting. They seem to ignore all physical characteristics, so we never quite understand what draws one dog to any other in particular. However, we can be sure it has nothing to do with the kinds of prejudices we impose on other people—prejudices we rarely, fortunately, impose on dogs themselves. Us/them, we/they, and in-group/out-group are categories we can certainly teach our dogs (a dog can learn to attack somebody of a specific color, for instance). But fortunately we don't usually want to. It is much better to learn from dogs their egalitarian tendencies than to impose our divisive ones on them. The photos in this book are a testament to this.

At no point in history has there been as great an interest in dogs from the scientific community as there is right now. Whole laboratories at prestigious universities (Harvard's Cognitive Evolution Laboratory has just been renamed the Canine Cognition Laboratory) are being reconfigured to test the various abilities of dogs, and not just the kinds of faculties we have always granted them (smell, for example). Instead they are testing their *feelings*, a long-due recognition that when it comes to emotions, dogs may have a great deal to teach us. Could they not be our superiors when it comes to such complex positive feelings as friendship, empathy, and perhaps even love and compassion? This may sound like heresy to humans who are not besotted with their dogs, but for those of us who are, there is nothing humiliating in recognizing that they have abilities beyond our own. After all, nobody holds it against birds that they can fly. We know dogs can smell several orders of magnitude more than we can. Why should it surprise us that they may also have access to emotions we do not know? Or that the ones we know are more highly developed in dogs than in us? There is a line in the animated film *My Dog Tulip* that sums up what many people feel about their dogs: "She offered me what I had never found in my life with humans: constant, single-hearted, incorruptible, uncritical devotion, which it is in the nature of dogs to offer." No human is as constant, as uncritical, or finally as devoted as a dog. It is just part of their equipment, it is in their nature, it is what intrigues us, and it is what makes us, really, their emotional slaves. For nowhere else in nature are we faced with an animal whose capacity for love seems to surpass our own (there may well be such, but we are not in a position to observe it up close as we are with dogs).

The photographs of dogs by Art Wolfe in this book demonstrate one great truth that those of you who travel a great deal may have noticed as well. Is it not astonishing that all over the globe there are dogs? In every

Botswana. Kwando Reserve. African wild dogs (*Lycaon pictus*).

USA. Washington. Art and Wolfy.

South Asian Indian village I have ever visited, there were dogs. When I wandered around in the Uruguayan countryside, I saw dogs sleeping in front of estancias. They were in Bariloche in the mountains of Argentina and on the Pampas there as well. When I went to school in the Swiss mountains, they were on the ski slopes. When I studied Pali, the ancient Buddhist language, in Sri Lanka, I made friends with a dog by the Temple of the Tooth. When our family wandered in a huge outdoor market in Vietnam, a small dog attached himself to us and did not want to leave. It took all my persuasive powers to convince our boys that it would be hard to continue our trip around the world with this little charmer. I saw dogs in Bali. I saw them in the South of France and in northern Italy. I saw them in small rural hamlets in Germany and England and Portugal. Everywhere I have

visited in the world people live intimately with dogs. They love them; they trust them; they make them part of their daily lives. This has been true for the last fifteen thousand years at least. It is not likely to change in the next fifteen thousand either.

Art Wolfe and I share this sense of the importance of dogs both in our personal lives and in the life of the human species. Art's love for dogs is manifest in every one of his marvelous photographs. He grew up in the 1950s in Seattle in a family with three kids, five dogs, twenty-four chickens, plus goldfish, parakeets, and cats. He observes that he never knew a time when dogs were not part of his family and his life.

Art's favorite dog was Wolfy. (Isn't it appropriate that the photographer of this book is named Wolfe?) Wolfy joined his family when Art was a teen and they frequently headed out to the Cascades and Olympics to go hiking and fishing. Art always said that Wolfy was his best traveling partner.

Art started photographing people and their dogs in 1984 when he went to Tibet for the first time en route to Everest via the Northeast Ridge. At that time Lhasa was still very much a Buddhist and Tibetan city and, unlike today, it was still very remote. Art remembers that everything looked so different in town, even the dogs, and he started taking photos, beginning with roundish little kids with roundish little dogs.

Over the years, as Art traveled the world photographing wildlife and observing the vast diversity of human cultures, he could not help but notice that the special bond between humans and dogs was universal. From little hunting dogs in the forests of Venezuela to dogs accompanying Saharan herdsmen, they became a part of his observation of the world and the way he documents cultures, wild areas, and wild animals.

While no place on the planet is devoid of dogs, there are places such as Bali, India, and the Middle East where dogs are not accepted. Yet in many of Art's photos in this book, we see images of dogs and people—from those very cultures—that tell a different story. Think of the naked man with the arm and head ornaments (p. 23) holding the chin of a lovely, well-groomed dog. This is clearly a dog who is happy to be with this human and the feeling is clearly mutual. It is true that there are cultures where dogs are not liked; in fact they are regarded as unclean and most people avoid them (some even kick them or stone them). Yet in every such culture, without exception, there are many people who refuse to go along with this cultural taboo, and in fact do just the opposite. They seek dogs out. They bring them into their homes. They pat them; they walk with them; they seem to truly love them. No matter what their society tells them, they feel differently and cannot be talked out of their love of dogs. And how do the dogs in such cases react? Just as you would expect, they are delighted. They too show their true colors. Whereas normally in such a culture they will avoid people and skulk away, when they recognize somebody who likes them they open their hearts as wide as do the people. They become who they were meant to be.

We can see this in the photo of the sadhu, the Indian holy man (p. 30), with his cane and his holy drum and his orange turban and his many colorful beads. He is seated with a tiny puppy (obviously *his* puppy, for it wears an orange homemade collar), whose small head rests on the man's large foot. The puppy is devoted to the sadhu, and I bet the sadhu, whatever the villagers might say, is equally devoted to him. He would not take a step without him, and we can be sure it will be that way for the rest of both of their lives. We see the same sadhu in another photo, with the little pup sticking out his tiny pink tongue. Another sadhu, bare-chested with long white hair and a long white beard, has two dogs next to him, both looking extremely healthy and well-groomed (p. 38). Indians generally do not look kindly on dogs, but these people, and numerous others, obviously make exceptions. And look at the photo of the street dog in Bhutan (p. 34) with the woman holding his paw while the dog licks her nose. That woman does not care a fig what the rest of society says about this dog; she loves him.

In these photos we get to see dogs as they have become. That is, we see with our very own eyes how their nature has changed as they have gotten close to us. Think of the photo of the very wolflike dog in a Vietnamese courtyard (p. 160), with a rooster walking by. Descended from a carnivore who is always on the lookout for food—and is also at the top of the food chain—this dog simply looks pleased. Friends surround him. How did this happen? How did we change the nature of the beast so completely that he resembles, well, us? Of course, seen from a different angle, one could ask, How did the beast change our nature, such that natural carnivores as we may well once have been, are now best friends with a member of a different species?

We can see how much we have altered dogs' nature by observing the photos of people walking many dogs, as in the woman with the blue T-shirt walking six dogs on a single leash in Seattle (p. 119). She looks confident, and the dogs look thrilled to be where they are. They are not all from the same "clan" or "tribe"; that is for sure. Yet they all get along to the extent that they walk happily on a single lead, close by one another. Whatever natural aggression they may have felt in the presence of a "stranger" is now gone. There is also the photo set in Central Park (p. 134-135), where we can see eight calm dogs (and seven calm people). Same thing. Or look at the photo of the runners with their dogs eagerly awaiting the Furry 5K race, again in Seattle (p. 62). How did we do that? Did we breed their aggression away? Did we set an example by our own behavior? Did we just expect it and poof it was there? However we did it, we did it. Now if humans could only learn to be more like dogs!

In many of these photos we see a dog protecting his territory. Consider the large growling dog standing on boards (on a houseboat) in Vietnam, (p. 106). It is interesting to note that the territory is not just his; the territory is that of his human friends as well. There is of course nothing surprising in this. Except that when you think about it a bit more deeply, it *is* surprising, because it means that dogs have to engage in a rather sophisticated mental exercise. They must decide who "belongs" to them, and who does not belong. They must decide who is a friend, and who is a stranger. It is not instinctive. It is not as if the dog just knows from birth who his family is and who is not. He makes distinctions and he makes judgments, and these are based on his feelings. In fact, many a dog will *not* growl or bark at a stranger, because in his own private wisdom the dog has decided that *this* stranger is not really a stranger at all, but a potential friend. Fascinating fact: They are almost always right!

We know that children like dolls. Look at the photo of the little girl in Myanmar (p. 28) in her flowered dress holding a small pure white puppy as tenderly as she would any doll, or the boy with the colorful poncho in Peru holding a small brown and white puppy (p. 159), or the boys on p. 40 with their husky pups, or the picture of the two South American boys, each holding several puppies (p. 41). See the photo of the three small African children with the four squirming pups (p. 14)? Even the very youngest, who could not be more than a bit over a year, has already learned to cradle a puppy. I suspect that all children would rather hold a living puppy in their arms than a not-so-living doll. It is true that most children would be just as happy holding any small baby animal in their arms. But how many of these small animals would, like puppies, be as happy in the arms of a child as they are with their own mother?

Dogs only love us because we feed them. This is a myth we dog lovers hear all the time. It is part of the antidog catechism: They are but parasites, taking advantage of our credulity and need for love, pretending to be our friends merely to fill their bellies. Or we hear some similar variation of the notion that everything they do is purely instinct—that only we reason or feel. Of course this is especially true when it comes to the "higher" emotions, like love and friendship and altruism and empathy. So when we look at a photo like that of the Burmese monks (p. 154) with their pots (no doubt offerings of food from devoted laypeople), and we see the dogs patiently with half-closed eyes waiting, we think: Aha. They are there for the food. But if dogs were to observe humans in a restaurant, they could think the same. I love the picture of the African woman with her baby (p. 37), not so young anymore but still in a sling, holding a reluctant-looking puppy. Her breast is bare. We know there are societies where woman think nothing of sharing a bit of milk with a hungry pup.

And then there is trust. Somehow they trust us to do the right thing, and to do the safe thing. Look at the gorgeous photo of a man steering a canoe in Indonesia (p. 145) with three little children—and six trusting dogs. They know they are safe. Once again they have had to overcome a natural reluctance to get into a small tippy boat and be carried away on a river. But they easily do.

To see love flowing between two species is perhaps the closest we will ever come to a spiritual experience that is universal. In Art Wolfe's photograph of the Yanomamö man with the spotted dog (p. 140) and that of the children in the West African village holding the puppies in their laps (p. 14), we see evidence of the same feeling, the same deep pleasure in "otherness" that we can only have with a creature who returns the trust, the friendship, and the love. Dogs. Our species has been blessed.

Universal Declaration of the Rights of Dogs

The right to be adequately loved

The right to be adequately exercised

The right to be adequately fed

The right to fresh water

The right to be adequately housed

The right to engage in natural behavior

The right to friends and companions

The right to vote (just kidding)

The right to downtime

The right to medical care

The right to an easy death

The right to be free of experimentation

The right not to be eaten

The right to be free of exploitation

The right to play

The right to have one's emotional needs taken into consideration

The right to live in an interesting world (e.g., not confined to a backyard)

The right to be protected from harm by other dogs or people

LOVE

The oldest of all human/nonhuman bonds: dogs and us. We call it a bond, but it is more than that. Why not call it what it is? Love. People who have not lived with dogs don't always understand the depth of friendship that some of us have with this other species. It is not merely mutual affection, not that there's anything wrong with mutual affection. I share it with my cats, and have shared it with many other animals since childhood. People have felt affection for and from every imaginable animal, but mostly dogs, cats, birds, and horses. Some even manage to feel it for and from pigs and cows and sheep and ducks and chickens, the animals we raise on farms not for companionship but because of their caloric value. But dogs are different, because they can reciprocate not only with affection, but with true mutual friendship and mutual love. Here is another being who feels love as deeply as we do.

Dogs watch us. Dogs even stare at us, but not with the stare of a predator. They are looking at us as if seeing something in us that we ourselves sometimes miss: a capacity for love. That look, directly into our eyes, or

Benin. *(left)* In the midst of the geometric ochre mud huts of Taneka, daily life offers some beautiful and powerful scenes—women spinning yarn and processing cassava root, men tending cooking fires, and children playing with Basenji-like puppies.

our soul—it's as if they are waiting for us to acknowledge that capacity for love in ourselves. There are times when dogs seem to see our humanity far more clearly than we do, and this can enable us to reach for that place, to try to inhabit it, to attempt to become the person the dog in our life knows we secretly are.

Do we actually fall in love with dogs? The evidence in these photos from around the world would suggest it is true. Of course we do. And it is no less clear that dogs fall in love with us. The love is obvious to us and no amount of scientific skepticism will ever convince those of us who are on the receiving end to doubt the genuineness of canine love. We see it in their eyes: Dogs, more than any other animal, express their feelings in their eyes. The miracle is that everywhere on earth, across all cultures and continents, we read it so easily. But, alas, it is rarely personal: Dogs fall in love with anyone!

Is this a virtue or a shortcoming? Why not call it a virtue? When it comes to the ability to form instant friendships, dogs are our superiors. And when it comes to the ability to love unconditionally, dogs are definitely our superiors. Where else are they likely to surpass us? In their capacity for loyalty. It may sound like a cliché, but you will rarely encounter a person who has lived with a dog who does not express it. They also surpass us in their desire always to be close to us.

When we look at the photo of the three African children holding their four puppies (p. 14), what immediately stands out is how happy the puppies are to be held. True, they are squirming and posing and sniffing, but they clearly enjoy being touched by the children. And who can doubt that the children in their turn adore holding and stroking and playing with the puppies? Children in every culture are preprogrammed to love dogs, and love them they do. Children everywhere on earth feel great pleasure and pride in the sense of interspecies friendship that comes from being able to immediately bond with a puppy. And no animal permits this sense of interspecies friendship so reliably and so immediately as do dogs. When you see a small child playing with a puppy, you are watching the beginnings of altruism and compassion that will blossom into the greatest interspecies love story on the planet—that between dogs and humans!

USA. The bonds between children and dogs are strong. Here they have melded their considerable powers and persuaded the adults to pull them to Seattle's Alki Beach.

USA. This was a match made in heaven. When I saw this professional handler and his fantastic dreads, I knew what I had to do. I pulled him from one area of the showgrounds and the puli from another.

USA. Dogs will go faithfully, but sometimes reluctantly, where we lead. I love the body language evident on everyone's part in this photo.

USA. (*above*) A man enjoys time with his bulldogs. (*right*) A young woman hugs a poodle in San Francisco.

The love dogs express by licking us shows that we clearly

belong to their clan, and they to ours.

Indonesia. (*right*) Perhaps the oldest continuous farming society in the world, the Dani inhabit the once remote highlands of Irian Jaya, the Indonesian half of the island of New Guinea. Despite their fierce appearance, they are a friendly and welcoming culture. Dogs and pigs are the only domesticated animals in the Baliem Valley. Raids and ritual warfare were once a mainstay of Dani culture and the dogs sounded the alarm if anything was amiss.

USA. A man gathers up his westies after a romp in San Francisco's Golden Gate Park.

USA. A pair of red dachshunds are dressed in haute couture by their proud owner.

Dogs show no prejudice when it comes to friendship:

They like us short and tall, big and small, wide and thin.

They just like us, period.

Canada. Vancouver, British Columbia. Befeathered and bejeweled, a parade performer holds her tiny Chihuahua.

Lhasa, Tibet. (*above*) A toddler cradles a puppy in her parents' store. **Myanmar. Mandalay.** (*left*) A girl tenderly cradles a puppy.

Even a religious ascetic who has renounced the world

still has room in his heart for a dog.

India. (*left*) One of the seven holiest places to Hindus, Haridwar is home to the world's largest religious gathering every twelve years. The Kumbh Mela drew me and millions of others, including this sadhu, or holy man, with his prized bitch, adorned with a bindi, and pup from a recent litter.

USA. (*above*) The pathos of a golden retriever, especially an older one with a whitening face, is not to be denied.
Canada. (*right*) A big mixed-breed is at home in a crowd.

USA. (*above*) Whether or not dogs are helpmates to people living with disabilities, they certainly provide deep companionship and loyalty unlike any other relationships we have. **Bhutan. Bumthang Valley.** (*left*) Our canine friends are always looking for a connection and reward small kindnesses with pleasure.

Benin. (*above*) Boys play with a puppy in the village of Taneka. **Ethiopia.** (*right*) I first traveled to the Omo River to photograph for my book *Tribes*, a celebration of indigenous cultures around the world. It is an extremely isolated area and outside influences have been slow to encroach. The Mursi are a cattle-herding tribe, and Mursi women are famous for their huge lip plates, though this woman did not have one. When she realized I was going to photograph her, she stopped me and threaded some wildflowers through her earlobes. Through it all her little boy clutched at his puppy.

India. Haridwar, Uttarakhand. (*above/right*) Hindu sadhus sit with their dogs at their tents during the Kumbh Mela.

Mexico. Two boys proudly show off husky pups in Pátzcuaro.

Ecuador. Otavalo. Boys carry puppies for sale. Organizations such as Humane Society International are integral in promoting responsible animal ownership and the importance of spaying and neutering pets.

USA. Dogs outnumber people in this happy gathering.

USA. Seattle, Washington. A Chihuahua is happy to be in on the act.

USA. (*above*) A young rollerskater takes a break with her papillon. (*right*) Big and small, we love them all.

New Zealand. When in New Zealand, I had the privilege of filming the Pounamu, a Maori performing arts group, for my public TV show. A couple of the performers' children came with their pit bull terrier puppy. It was misty and cold and so they enjoyed the show wrapped together in a blanket.

Cuba. Like most other people, Cubans have a passion for dogs, whether purebred or mongrel. Here two boys play with their Dalmatian on the Malecón in Havana.

USA. A brace of poms and their human.

Japan. In a Kyoto pedestrian mall a proud owner of two poms shows off her charges.

All over the world, nobody, anywhere, can resist a puppy.
Nature has designed puppies to melt our hearts: the big eyes, the
snub nose, the floppy ears—there is even a scientific name
to describe these characteristics: "neoteny."

USA. A puppy, no bigger than a handful, is coddled in Seattle, Washington.

PLAY

Wherever there are dogs, there are dogs playing. It's not just puppies who play, but adult dogs as well. So do dogs in Tibet or Mongolia or China play differently than dogs in Paris or New York City? It seems that dog play is universal. Dogs everywhere play in the same way, and more important still, they play with humans in the same way. Tibetan herdsmen will throw a stick for a dog to fetch just as surely as will a villager in the Andes in Peru and a little girl in the Scottish Highlands.

Dogs are the ne plus ultra of play. Perhaps no other animal anywhere in the world plays as consistently, as readily, as eagerly, and as fairly as dogs. With each other, and with us, they are ready to play at a moment's notice. They will handicap themselves to adjust to our less adroit ways. And, most remarkably, if they make a mistake playing with another dog, they will offer a brief apology (by play bowing) and request that the game continue. Just how sophisticated their play behavior can be is only recently coming under scientific scrutiny. True, dog play may not be chess, but then chess may not be play: Some might consider it war in disguise. No matter where in the world, dog play is never about winning; it is about the sheer enjoyment of the game.

USA. (*left*) An athletic disc dog snatches a Frisbee from high in the air.

Dogs and Frisbees: a marriage made in gadget heaven. Who would have supposed? I love the picture of the dog five feet off the ground (p. 52) with the Frisbee in his mouth. Now, do these dogs think they are catching a bird? Of course not. Dogs are not stupid. They know it is play, and play that delights both them and us. Look at the photo of the woman holding three Frisbees (p. 63) with her dog on top of her back, anticipating her next move. Strange place to be? Not at all: It is all in fun. Dogs surf, they skateboard, they ride on motorcycles; the trick is to start them out early.

Play is still somewhat mysterious. Consider when you throw a stick for your dog, and she runs to retrieve it. She brings it back, but instead of dropping it at your feet, she drops at your feet and begins to shred the stick. You reach down and she growls, warning you away. Then she leaps to her feet and races away with the stick, hoping you will chase her so she can dexterously avoid you. Then she will lie down and continue destroying the stick all over again. It is all in fun. The growl is not a real growl. The running away is not really running away. The shredding is not really shredding. Call it metaplay. She is playing with play. It is a reversal. Normally, the "retriever" retrieves for you. (You shoot the bird—heaven forbid, but that is the origin—and she races over, remembers to keep a soft mouth, and brings the dead bird back to you as she has been trained to do.) But here your dog is saying, "The hell with that. You have your idea of play. I have mine." And hers is to destroy the prize, to show you that she can, that she can defy you. Of course she is not really defying you. She is just playing at defiance. That is what makes it so enchanting. She knows that you know that she knows it is all in fun. Most of the time, too, you get it and play along: You stamp your foot and demand the return of the stick (when she knows that you know that she knows it is all just a charade— you don't really expect her to relinquish the stick). Then she growls and bites harder, woofs at you and races away, knowing you will make a pointless attempt to catch her—thrilled at how clumsy you really are and how slow she knows you to be!

Canada. Toronto, Ontario. More and more cities are making sections of their parks available as off-leash areas for dogs and their humans. For many communities it has become a quality-of-life issue. Here dogs gambol on the shores of Lake Ontario.

Dogs everywhere play, as part of their very nature.

USA. (*right*) Most dogs have their owners jumping through hoops.

USA. (*above*) The Venice boardwalk in southern California is a playground for everyone.
(*left*) An alternative way of taking the daily constitutional in Seattle's Fremont neighborhood.

Dogs play football, or soccer,

or any other game you ask them to.

Teamwork is in their DNA.

Ecuador. This is a familiar scene everywhere in the world: a boy with a soccer ball takes a rest from playing with his dog in a field near Quito.

USA. (*above*) Frisbee or disc dogs combine an amazing amount of intelligence, athleticism, discipline, and training into one sport. Here the handler and dog have to be a perfect working unit in performing an intricately choreographed two-minute routine. (*left*) Events like Seattle Animal Shelter's Furry 5K raise hundreds of thousands of dollars to help pay for the care and adoption of stray and owner-surrendered animals.

Brazil. Proud of his rocky prize, a dog parades, tail held high, in the streets of the small village of Santo André.

USA. San Francisco. Westies at play.

The odd thing is that humans don't chase sticks, and don't see the purpose. But when we see the pure joy it gives to our dogs, we get into the fun of it. Once they start chasing sticks, dogs have found their purpose in life.

USA. Marblemount, Washington. A Leonberger launches itself after a stick.

Canada. Toronto, Ontario. A yellow lab fetches a stick from the cold waters of Lake Ontario.

Kenya. A pup plays with a stick at Mpala Ranch. In addition to being a Smithsonian research center, Mpala is host to international researchers studying wildlife ecology, conservation and management, and economic sustainability of local livelihoods.

STREETWISE

There are dogs all over the world who live on the street. I call them streetwise, because otherwise they would not last long. These are dogs who for whatever reason have been cut loose from their human homes, and are on their own. Life for such dogs is not easy: We think they can revert to their wild nature easily, but this is probably a fallacy. After all, dogs have lived with humans for so many thousands of years that it is in their genetic makeup to be dependent upon us.

On the other hand, one advantage of street life for dogs is that they are with other dogs. They have a pack, often quite a substantial one, and packs are interesting social phenomena, especially for the dogs in them. Life in a pack is rarely boring. The social complexity of the relations within these packs can be elaborate, and solving the many problems that arise can take a certain kind of intelligence that is sometimes dormant when dogs are pampered in our homes. Whenever I see street dogs I believe I can see a certain supplication in their eyes, a dim hope that they will be rescued from this difficult life and taken back into the human family.

Mexico. Michoacán. (*left*) In the week leading up to the Day of the Dead holiday in Pátzcuaro, families gather for prayer and remembrance of departed family members. They clean and decorate cemeteries and churches and they bring their dogs with them as part of the family.

India. Haridwar, Uttarakhand. (*above*) On a high stoop in a narrow street a dog sits sentinel at a business entrance. **Kolkata. West Bengal.** (*right*) Two men hang out on a Kolkata street. Whether the dog was theirs or just wanting human companionship and a meal is unknown.

India. Jaisalmer, Rajasthan. (*above*) In the heart of the Thar Desert, the ancient city of Jaisalmer is home to street dogs and pampered pets alike. Brazil. (*left*) Bahian street dogs are no cause for alarm, although the mule seems unsure. It is impossible to know whether these were strays or escaped dogs out on a neighborhood jaunt.

In every culture throughout the world,

even those where dogs are not appreciated,

there are people who love dogs.

Bhutan. Thimphu. In this remote Himalayan kingdom where gross national happiness
is measured instead of gross national product, the street dog population has boomed. People
officially don't own the dogs, but neighborhoods band together to feed them. Over the decades,
less-than-ideal measures have been taken to reduce the numbers. Now Humane Society
International is working with government officials to spay/neuter and
vaccinate close to fifty thousand dogs throughout the country.

Mexico. Pátzcuaro, Michoacán. A dog drinks from a flower can during the preparations for the Day of the Dead.

Bhutan. Bumthang Valley. Owned by none and owned by all, Bhutanese street dogs radiate a rare peace.

India. Varanasi. Uttar Pradesh. (*above*) In India most free-roaming dogs are related to the Pariah dog, an ancient feral canine of Asia and Africa. Some are abandoned pets, some are pets of slumdwellers, and the survivors are very savvy street dogs who have learned to fend for themselves. There are nonprofits and governmental agencies working to control dog populations in humane ways through spay/neuter and adoption programs as well as educational programs for humans. **Mexico.** (*left*) A colorful city of elegant colonial architecture, San Miguel de Allende is a World Heritage Site. Dogs sit at ornately carved courtyard doors and bark at passersby from balustraded balconies.

WORK

When some people hear the term "working dog" they immediately think of humans exploiting an animal, the way we so obviously do with farm animals who are there because they serve our purpose. But dogs are not here because they serve our purpose. Well, not exclusively. And while most of them do nothing more than simply provide unparalleled companionship, there are dogs, especially in the non-Western world, who work for a living. I have seen them, and I have talked to the people who work with them, and it does seem a counterintuitive truth, but dogs like to work. This may be because the work they do is associated with certain drives, talents, and desires native to dogs in any event, which we simply modify for our human purposes. I am thinking of dogs who assist in hunting, for example. Dogs come from wolves, which are superb cooperative hunters. They do it well and efficiently, and they clearly enjoy themselves in the process. So it is perhaps not surprising that hunting dogs take pride in their work and get pleasure from it. But is this inevitably true?

New Zealand. (*left*) While filming *Art Wolfe's Travels to the Edge*, I met up with a shepherd on the South Island. His dogs are brilliant technicians, reacting with precision and excitement to his whistles. It is no secret that there are more sheep in New Zealand than people, so canine workers are critical in moving the herds from range to range, preserving the bounty of the pastureland in the process.

What about dogs who guard sheep? Well, here too we have simply harnessed an innate drive: Wolves guard their fellow wolves, especially their young. Guard dogs such as the immense and muscular Anatolian shepherd dog (also known as Karabash, Turkish for "black head") who guard flocks of sheep from wolves and other predators—and even from cheetahs in Africa—are raised from birth with sheep. It is not that they think they are sheep (although some people believe they do) but that they recognize the sheep as part of the pack, to be protected. Do they like what they do? I think they probably do. They certainly take it seriously.

I have seen many working dogs on farms, and there can be little doubt about how excited herding dogs become as they do their work. Their tongues hang out in that exuberant way that suggests a human smile, their tails wag, and they just seem to be unable to get enough of the work. I always find it a bit sad that in many farming communities around the world the dogs are not allowed into the house. Farmers say this "spoils" them, but I don't believe it for a minute. They would do the same work, with the same enthusiasm, no matter where they slept. But surely they would enjoy the intimacy of their human friends in the evening after a hard day's work, lying at their feet by a roaring fire. What would be wrong with this?

Dogs have been hunting and guarding and herding for thousands of years. But what about the newer forms of work for dogs? Acting as guide dogs for the blind is perhaps the best known of the services that dogs now provide. There are also hearing dogs who assist people who are deaf. There are service dogs who help people in wheelchairs, dogs who allow children to read to them, and therapy dogs who go into hospitals, hospices, and nursing homes. There are seizure-alert dogs, police dogs, drug-sniffing dogs, and rescue dogs. Dogs work wherever they are needed—in prisons, in schools, and in hospitals. It seems we are finding new work all the time for these versatile, cheerful, willing laborers. How do they feel about it? Dogs are hypersocial, so if they are given the reward of human company, that seems to be practically all they wish for, as long as the human companion loves them. But the failure rate is about 50 percent, and that has remained pretty steady over time. Half of all dogs trained for this work just don't make the grade, usually because they are unwilling to perform. (My own dog Benjy is a primary example. He was a colossal failure in spite of his pedigree, elaborate training, etc. He just did not want to work.) They are never mean about it (that is not in the nature of most dogs). But some would, like Melville's Bartleby the scrivener, simply "prefer not to."

USA. Graduating more than ten thousand teams since its founding in 1942, Guide Dogs for the Blind has provided at no cost a means for enhanced mobility and companionship for legally blind people.

New Zealand. Herding dogs are all business.

USA. In Washington's sage country, a research biologist keeps company with his Brittany spaniel for long hours as he uses radio telemetry to locate and track the endangered Greater sage grouse.

USA. (*above*) When I spotted this police officer and his German shepherd in Santa Monica, California, I wasn't carrying a camera, which is a rarity for me. He showed utmost patience while I ran back to my car, retrieved equipment, and returned to photograph him. His shepherd is a trained explosives-detection dog. (*left*) On the corner near Seattle's famous Pike Place Market, a homeless man panhandles. With a dog and two cats, who probably came from animal shelters, he gains companionship not found in his human brethren.

Dogs smell a world we can only intuit.

USA. (*right*) The precision and efficiency of dogs' noses has been put to terrific use in conservation and research efforts on a diverse array of threatened and endangered species including tigers, spotted owls, caribou, and jaguars. These dogs are trained by Conservation Canines to detect scat from these particular animals, and then the DNA is analyzed from the scat to determine species, sex, even individual identities. The ideal dog for this program usually is found at the local animal shelter; these dogs are obsessive and extremely high-energy, making them difficult to maintain as a family pet. It's a win-win situation when one of these intensely focused dogs is adopted to help save the Earth's wildlife.

Mongolia. (*above*) At their summer encampment near the Siberian border, Tsaatan children ride and herd their livelihood, the reindeer. (*right*) Tsaatan translates to "people of the reindeer." Reindeer provide food, clothing, and transportation for this endangered people. Here large dogs are essential to protect the critical herds from wolves.

Myanmar. (*above*) Oxcarts are a chief form of local transport in Bagan, towing tourists and locals alike to the amazing temples and pagodas of the ancient city. Trotting back and forth along the dusty track, dogs are a constant accompaniment. **USA.** (*right*) This Iditarod musher and his dogs run thousands of miles a year, but all the work only makes them stronger and more excited to run! I got three chances and about thirty seconds with them before they hurtled out of sight into the forest. The light early winter snowfall on the logging road in the Washington Cascades made it impossible for him to stop and pull his dogs around.

Brazil. Pantaneiros ready their mules to move cattle to higher ground in Brazil's Pantanal. The cowboys and their herds coexist with a dense population of wildlife in the world's largest wetland. A boxer is on the scene to protect from predators and even does some herding.

Mongolia. A horseman takes off across the vast Northern Steppe. The land of Genghis Khan manages to retain its rich traditional horse and herding culture.

Chile. (*above*) South American cowboys—gauchos—herd cattle, sheep, and horses. As with all traditional herdsmen, dogs are an indispensable part of their lives. The gauchos wear heavy woolen ponchos, garments originally created by ancient peoples of the Andes to keep warm from the howling Patagonian wind and dry during rain and snowfall. **Bhutan.** (*right*) Herding dogs nap as they await their next task on a farm in the Paro Valley.

Argentina. (*above*) A gaucho and his trusted dog drive sheep across the rugged Patagonian steppe near Los Glaciares National Park. **Mexico. Guanajuato.** (*right*) A young man delivers firewood to the homes in San Miguel de Allende. The firewood is strapped to uncomplaining donkeys who are, in turn, kept in line by a dog.

China. (*above*) The Pamir Plateau is a mountainous knot in Central Asia from which the five great mountain ranges of Asia radiate: the Himalaya, Karakoram, Hindu Kush, Tien Shan, and Kunlun Shan. The plateau provides ample forage for small herds of goats, sheep, camels, and yaks. Having spent the summer months in the high mountain valleys, herders with the invaluable aid of their dogs lead their livestock down the mountains ahead of winter's onslaught.

Mali. (*left*) In the Sahara Desert Tuareg tribesmen gather to water their herds. Their dogs are lithe, fast, and have a strong guarding instinct.

Myanmar. Near the ancient city of Bagan women and children and their
dogs herd goats. The goats are raised for meat and milk.

104

Vietnam. Ha Long Bay. (*above*) A guard dog shows his ferocity by chewing on a rope as we float too near for his comfort. (*right*) Famous for its precipitous limestone cliffs, thousands of islands, and rich biodiversity, Ha Long Bay has been inhabited by humans since prehistoric times. And with humans come dogs. Living on floating fishing villages, people have dogs to guard their families and possessions.

Dogs did not evolve to work for us, but they love to.

Vietnam. Ha Long Bay. A dog patrols the deck of a fisherman's houseboat.

PAMPERED

There are people who believe we spoil our dogs. We insist on celebrating their birthdays (a concept decidedly foreign to the canine birthday boy or girl), or dressing them up (the vote is not yet in whether they find this humiliating), or, if they are small enough, carrying them around in our arms (this definitely pleases them), or putting them in a carriage (this pleases them less, I am sure), or taking them on long drives into the country (this has got to be one of a dog's favorite pastimes), or having a picnic with and for them ("yes, yes, yes," they say). We make certain they are not too cold or too hot, and we give them the best medical care we can afford, and sometimes even that we can ill afford. Some of us cook for them. Some give up half or more of our bed for them. Those who do not love dogs are baffled. The rest of us find it entirely self-evident why we would do such things.

We often hear that non-Western societies are more realistic, and therefore do not pamper dogs. Well, just take a look at the photo of the cool dude with his equally cool dog (p. 39). (Can dogs be self-conscious? Do they know how cool they look? I think so.) This sadhu from India would be right at home in Brooklyn. In India, holy men (sadhus) are supposed to be beyond possessions. The sadhus we see here, though, are still mired in "maya," with a sense of "yours" and "mine." Those are *his* dogs.

USA. (*left*) The camouflage backpack offers a rugged presentation for this pampered pom.

Some cultures, it is true, are more besotted with dogs than others. Take France, for example. Walk into any good gourmet restaurant in Paris and you are likely to share the space with a well-mannered, elaborately manicured dog. Your neighbor will have as a dinner companion his or her dog. Nobody finds this objectionable. In fact, it isn't. Dogs learn their restaurant manners, and they also learn to like good French cuisine. When you leave the restaurant and get into a taxi, you are likely to find two people sitting in the front seat: the driver, and his or her canine companion. A guaranteed way to reach the taxi driver's heart is to ask about the dog. I did that often, and was told that the dogs love driving! They look out the window (searching, naturally, for other dogs), take in the sights, and offer opinions on backseat customers. The French find it normative, and I began to love it.

No dog is without the potential to be the best friend to some human. So when people think we are pampering or spoiling our dogs beyond what they deserve, they are not aware that this deep friendship works in both directions—from them to us and from us to them. People who say we pamper dogs really mean that we are "spoiling" them. Is it really possible to spoil a dog? We can spoil children, definitely, but in pampering dogs we are just giving them the full attention, and love, they deserve. After all, that is what they do for us—give us their full attention and love—every moment of their lives.

Canada. (*right*) Events like the Pride Parades in Seattle and Vancouver have become family events which include dogs. These participants were celebrating the life of the dog who was no longer with them.

Do dogs like to be washed? Do they like to smell nice?

Do they like to please their human companions?

Yes, yes, and yes.

USA. Marymoor Park, Washington. (*right*) The Wash Spot in Marymoor Park is an ingenious self-service dog-cleaning business next to the off-leash area in the park. Self-service dog-cleaning businesses are becoming ever-more popular. It's yet another way to indulge the pups and keep the house smelling fresh.

Japan. (*above*) A Yorkie gets ready for a ride on a moped through Tokyo streets. Japan is a pet-crazy country outdoing nearly everyone when it comes to the essence of pampered and cute. **USA. New York, New York.** (*left*) Two pugs give their opinion of the weather.

Dogs take such pleasure being out and about examining the real world, even if it means at the end of a leash with a dog they hardly know next to them. Their mood is always up the minute they are out!

USA. (*right*) The sight of a professional dogwalker with a legion of charges is commonplace in big cities. Many modern dogs have quite the schedule with their various service providers—the dogwalker, the groomer, the psychiatrist. But seriously, beware that your dog doesn't love the walker more than you!

118

USA. (*above*) Two poodles beg at their favorite bakery in New York. Unfortunately, it was closed at the time. **England.** (*left*) Three little dogs in a pram shill for their owner on a London street. Behind them is a crank organ which will be played for a few pence. Not the first time cute dogs have been used to increase business!

Canada. A dachshund and his doting human.

Canada. A double-loved dog in Vancouver, British Columbia.

Dog breeds are important to humans, but not to the dogs themselves.

They make none of the distinctions we make among ourselves.

High dog, low dog, giant dog, miniature dog, white dog, black dog—for dogs,

all dogs are just dogs. They are all potential friends.

USA. Dog shows are a great place to learn about different breeds from tiny to massive, such as these small Pomeranians and supersized Leonberger.

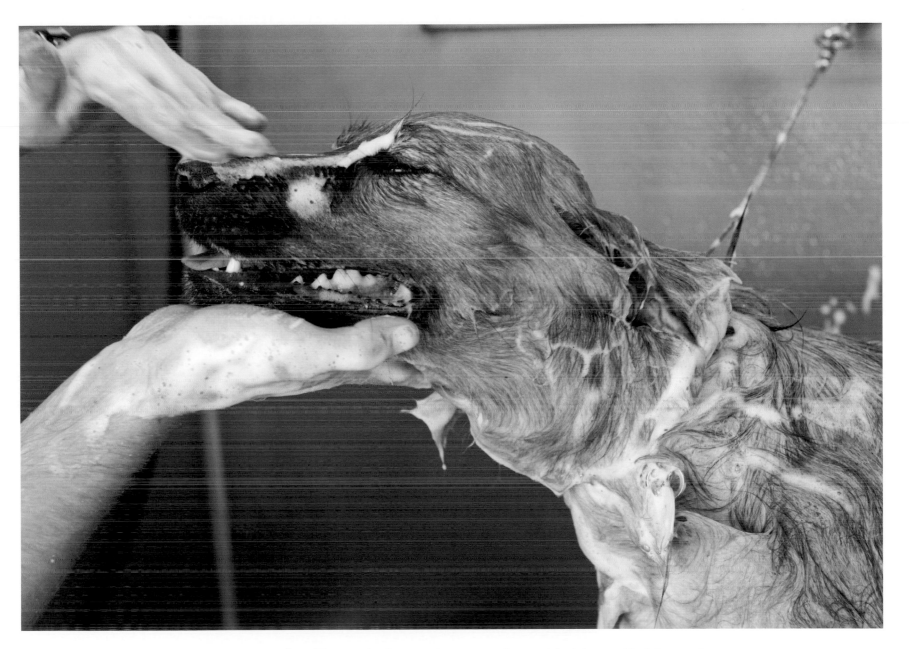

USA. Washington. (*above*) Saturated with soap and water, a good-natured dog is happy with all the attention.

(*left*) As evidenced by their steady gazes, greyhounds are sight hounds.

Morocco. Marrakesh. (*above*) In some cultures dogs aren't as accepted, but there are fanciers in every society.

USA. (*right*) Ready for the show ring, a schnauzer has been buffed, brushed, and trimmed to perfection.

Dogs care about how they look, but probably in a different way than we do. They know when they are feeling clean and healthy. Beautiful? In the eyes of the human observer only!

USA. (*above*) Dog in tow, a recumbent cyclist hits the road on his cross-country journey near Grand Teton National Park, Wyoming. (*left*) Looking cool in a sidecar and doggles!

USA. New York, New York. (*above*) A little dog commands the sidewalk in the Big Apple. **Washington.** (*left*) Proof of the extent to which dogs have taken over our lives, two papillons have commandeered a stroller.

USA. Central Park, New York. In a scene that repeats itself in many American cities, apartment-dwelling urban dogs romp in the park as their owners socialize. Dog ownership and friendship go hand in hand. How many long term relationships get their start in the dog park?

USA. (*above*) The purse dog is hardly a modern phenomenon. In imperial times, wealthy Chinese would carry miniature Pekingese dogs in their voluminous sleeves. (*right*) A tiny Chihuahua peeks from a plush carrier.

USA. Mt. Vernon, Washington. (*above*) An Afghan hound is readied for the ring. (*left*) Thousands of dog shows take place around the world annually. From small to large, they judge the conformational standards for purebred dogs and fan our fascination with dogs. The first modern show was in England in 1859, and since then the domestic dog has been categorized and refined into hundreds of breeds.

DOGS AROUND THE WORLD

There is no part of the world where humans live that has not also been colonized by dogs. I know there is bound to be an exception *somewhere* on our planet, but Art Wolfe and I have yet to find it. When early humans took canoes and left for an unknown destination, they took dogs with them. Yes, it is possible that the dogs were taken along as food, but soon they transcended their function as a source of calories. They would guard the new villages; they would sound the alarm when a stranger, human or animal, approached. Some were eventually allowed into the home, however reluctantly at first, and eventually they proved their value: They ate the scraps, they kept the children warm at night, and they continued to act as guards. But at the same time they provided companionship to the entire household. That companionship grew over the years, so that everywhere in the world, even in those societies where dogs, for whatever reason, were not loved or cherished or even accepted, there were always some people who did love them and did wish to be with them, and took them into their lives as their most beloved friends. This seems to be what dogs want more than anything else—to be with their person. It seems to be their very raison d'être: Dogs live to live with us, everywhere in the world.

Venezuela. *(left)* When I was working on my book *Tribes*, I went through the extensive permissions process with the Venezuelan government and traveled to the remote Sierra Parima to photograph the sylvan Yanomamö people. Taking great pride in his appearance, this skilled huntsman donned ceremonial dress for both himself and his special hunting bitch, enhancing her buff-colored coat with spots of charcoal. The dogs are indispensable helpmates in flushing and catching tapirs, agouti, and peccaries—critical sources of protein for a people living at subsistence levels.

Bhutan. Dogs trot across a bridge festooned with prayer flags in the Paro Valley.

Dogs delight in the hunt, but they take even more pleasure in just being around their human friends.

Do dogs like to walk in the rain? If they are walking with their person, they are happy whatever the weather.

USA. (*left*) The daily constitutional is taken, rain or shine, in New York City.

147

China. (*above*) In Lhasa a child drinks milk in the company of the family dog. The most well known Tibetan dog breed is the small Lhasa apso, once bred in Buddhist monasteries as a sentinel dog. **Bhutan. Phobjika Valley.** (*right*) A privileged dog peeks through an elaborately painted window at the Gangteng Monastery.

Indonesia. Irian Jaya. A dog tries to ingratiate itself with a circle of Dani men.

India. A small merchant in Delhi keeps shop with his son and dog.

Are dogs religious? They seem to have a sense of the sacred:

Play is sacred, their love for us is sacred, and finally,

they seem to have a love for the whole world.

Just like a good Buddhist monk.

Bhutan. Monks, brilliant in carmine robes, meditate near a wall of prayer wheels.

Myanmar. (*above*) At a monastery in Mandalay dogs patiently wait, with tails wagging, for handouts as monks clean up after a meal. **Bhutan.** (*right*) Waiting for handouts, dogs roam the streets of Paro.

Dogs show no prejudice toward the aged.

They will adjust their pace for anyone. We are their best friends,

whatever our status.

Bhutan. Paro Valley. Bhutanese society is extremely traditional and the country was once one of the most isolated in the world. Maintaining harmony between ancient and modern is a difficult balancing act.

Ethiopia. Omo River. (*above*) A Mursi girl holds a puppy close to her breast. **Peru.** (*right*) A Quechua youth holds a puppy beneath a rainbow blanket fastened as a poncho in Cusco.

Ecuador. Otavalo. (*above*) Otavaleños are famous for their woven goods. An indigenous woman sits and spins yarn with her child and a dog curled at her feet for warmth. **Vietnam. Ninh Binh.** (*left*) A mother passes a quiet moment with her child at home.

Sometimes you just need to take shelter from the storm.

USA. Seattle, Washington. (*right*) A couple and their dog take refuge under a Japanese maple on a rainy autumn day in the Washington Park Arboretum.